Always—Only—One

By Robert Wolfe

Karina Library Press
2013

Always—Only—One:
A Dialogue with the Essence of Nondual India

Robert Wolfe

ISBN-13: 978-1-937902-12-4 (paperback)

Karina Library Press
PO Box 35
Ojai, California 93024

Editor: Michael Lommel

Special thanks to Tom Burt
for help in producing this manuscript

Also by Robert Wolfe

Print and ebook

Living Nonduality:
Enlightenment Teachings of Self-realization

The Gospel of Thomas:
The Enlightenment Teachings of Jesus

One Essence:
The Nondual Clarity of an Ancient Zen Poem

Science of the Sages:
Scientists Encountering Nonduality from Quantum Physics to
Cosmology to Consciousness

Elementary Cloudwatching:
31 Meditations on Living without Time

Small ebooks

Enduring Enrichment

The Absolute Enigma

Where does infinity lead?

www.livingnonduality.org

You are not being instructed to shut your eyes to this world. You are only to know yourself first, and then see the whole world as the Self.

...

*The Self is unlimited, and is not confined to the body. There is **always only one**, and that is the Self.*

Ramana Maharshi

Preface

The core of this book is a commentary on the pertinent enlightenment verses of the Ashtavakra Gita as found in the vernacular translation made by Swami Nityaswarupananda for publication in 1953. It also collates the essentials of the teachings of the Diamond Sutra, the Mandukya Upanishad, and, as if in dialogue with the question, How can I be Self-realized?, selectively collates quotes from Ramana Maharshi on several key related themes of his nondual teachings. I consider these to be the essence of the rich literature of India springing from genuine nondual awareness.

I have sometimes paraphrased the wording for brevity or emphasis or to more nearly configure with modern language. I find it helpful also to sometimes put a word in quotes to show it is being used in a nonstandard sense and better convey its meaning. The Reference guide at the end of the book provides references for the original source quotes (in translation; this includes Ramana whose native language was Tamil).

Please note that while the word "he" has been used in these texts to reference the sage, the word "she" is equally applicable.

Of the various Vedic teaching texts (or *gita* in Sanskrit) the one you've most likely heard quoted, aside from the venerable Bhagavad Gita, is the Ashtavakra Gita.

Sometimes called Ashtavakra Samhita, it may predate both the Bhagavad Gita and the Buddha.

The Ashtavakra describes a person's state of being who has transcended the limitations of the relative and divisive viewpoint of duality. It elucidates the principles of the enlightened perspective known contemporarily in the West as *nonduality*. Like other gitas, it aims to reveal the rudiments of a universal, unlimited condition of being, in which individual objects and conceptions all take form.

The words of the Ashtavakra may finally render any words meaningless—since the hearing of the words themselves, born from insight, may immediately communicate the absolute actuality in its essence.

Such spiritual luminaries as Ramana Maharshi, Vivekananda and Ramakrishna have dipped from the Ashtavakra Gita's well of wisdom. Neem Karoli Baba deemed it "the purest of scriptures."

Not surprisingly, there have been numerous translations of and commentaries on the Ashtavakra over the centuries.

Many of them are out of print. Most of the ones I refer to here, however, are currently available.

The late Ramesh Balsekar, a successor to the advaita teacher Nisargadatta, wrote a partial commentary (a couple of decades ago), *A Duet of One*. He said the Ashtavakra Gita "provides an astonishingly direct, positive and unequivocal exegesis of the doctrine of nonduality, perhaps the best that has ever been done. ...the Truth, the whole Truth, and nothing but the Truth."

Shortly after Balsekar's book, the Indian guru Osho published *Discourses on the Great Mystic Ashtavakra*, and said of the gita: "Before it the Vedas pale, the Upanishads are a mere whisper. Even the Bhagavad Gita does not have the majesty found in the Ashtavakra Gita—it is simply unparalleled."

A third Indian commentator since, Swami Chinmayananda (*Discourses on Astavakra Gita*—an alternate spelling of Ashtavakra), said it "directly points out the way and the goal...can show light and can serve as a true guide...to the spiritual Reality behind life and its expressions."

There is a modern translation of the Ashtavakra Gita by Thomas Byrom, Ph.D.: *The Heart of Awareness*. Its foreword by a Sanskrit and Vedic scholar describes the text as "the outpourings of a realized individual."

Byrom says of the Ashtavakra Gita, "This is not speculative philosophy.... We are all one Self.... Everything else is an illusion: the little self, the world, the universe. All these things arise with the thought 'I,' that is, with the idea of separate identity.... But our true nature is pure and choiceless awareness. We are already and always fulfilled."

And of the presumed author of the Gita, Byrom notes: "We not only know next to nothing about him, we cannot even be sure when he lived.... And it is entirely appropriate that the real master of the Gita remain forever unknown since, as he has Ashtavakra say of himself, 'for what he has become, there is no name'.... Within the ever-fulfilled and ubiquitous Self, there is no place for these—or any—distinctions."

The commentaries aside, there are also several versions of the text itself. Available on the internet is a translation by John Richards. A somewhat extended version also by Richards is at the website www.realization.org.

In Bart Marshall's book, *The Perennial Way*, there is a fluid version which he compiled from extant English translations (several other enlightenment classics are also gathered together in Marshall's book). Marshall describes the Gita: "Every word is aimed at triggering Self-realization—no suggestions for self-improvement, no guidelines for moral behavior, no practical wisdom for daily life."

Perhaps the most authoritative translation available is *Ashtavakra Samhita* by Swami Nityaswarupananda, originally issued around 1930. There are copious explanatory footnotes for terms such as "Absolute," and an index for such topics as

"Self." His commentary is suitable but is as sporadic as the gita's verses themselves.

In the introduction to the book, the Swami says the Ashtavakra Gita "is not a philosophical treatise...on the contrary, an unfoldment of the ultimate Truth...[concerning] dualism as an unmitigated illusion..."

He describes the Gita's emphasis:

> The unity of the Self with all that exists is realized. In fact, nothing exists but the Self...
>
> When the Self is realized as the only reality, difference and distinction vanish like the mist before the sun, and freedom is attained.
>
> In reality, the Self is always free and freedom is not attained, but simply realized and discovered. The impediment to self-realization and freedom is our pre-occupation with the objective world, which inevitably leads to conflict of interests...
>
> All things other than the Self are only an appearance, no matter how ever persistent and consistent some of them may appear to be.
>
> The Self alone is real, and all not-Self is appearance. The psychological world is as much an illusionary appearance as the objective world.

The 298 verses of the Ashtavakra Gita cross twenty chapters, with as few as four verses in several of the chapters, to as many as one hundred verses in Chapter 18.

The Gita is structured as a dialogue between a king, Janaka, and an adept of *advaita* or nondual realization named Ashtavakra (*advaita* means "not two" in Sanskrit). For the Gita's instructive purposes, Janaka poses queries which

Ashtavakra responds to at length, with much detail and repetition. His replies sometimes range far from the question.

Janaka's first question is the primal one: how can I too be Self-realized? Ashtavakra takes nineteen verses (to the end of Chapter 1) to answer Janaka's question.

Chapter 2 begins with Janaka declaring that Ashtavakra's previous words have transmitted the clarity he had been seeking. To illustrate this, he utilizes two dozen verses (concluding the chapter) to express the nondual realization of which he is now aware.

But Chapter 3 begins with Ashtavakra challenging the king as to whether he will be capable of applying the precepts of Self-realization—such as non-attachment—in his daily life. This takes up all fourteen verses of Chapter 3. In Chapters 4 through 6, Ashtavakra continues by describing what enlightenment has meant to him, in his life, in terms of the nondual perspective.

Throughout Chapter 7, king Janaka assures the sage that his illumination is thoroughgoing. Ashtavakra then expands on the details of the teachings (Chapters 8 through 11). The king responds by confirming his commitment to these teachings, whatever that might entail (through Chapter 14).

Ashtavakra then gives a few deeper meanings to some of the precepts, and reaffirms many of the points stated earlier. This consumes Chapters 15, 16, 17 and all of the one hundred verses of Chapter 18. "Chapter 18 is like the last chapter of *Bhagavad-Gita*, a resume of the previous teachings." (Swami Nityaswarupananda)

In the final two chapters, Janaka is grateful for the generosity of Ashtavakra's instruction, and confirms once again that his enlightenment has been profound.

So, aside from the couple of conversational exchanges, virtually everything that is said in this gita is from the standpoint of nondual awareness, whether spoken by the enlightened sage or the enlightened king. In that context, if you read "he said," it would matter little which one said it. Byrom notes, "The Gita has only one voice…uncompromised clarity."

My interpretive commentary, which follows here, is not intended to be a scholarly treatment. It is, instead, a means for a composite understanding (for those unfamiliar with the precepts of nonduality, née advaita) concerning the relevance of Self-realization to the lives of inquiring readers.

In order to comprehend the message of the Ashtavakra, let's consider an outline of the nondual teaching, as it has been expressed by many diverse exponents over the millenia.

All spiritual and religious traditions have had in common a contemplation of a fundamental actuality (or factor, or condition), beyond which there is not anything else. The words and names used to indicate or define this ultimate actuality demonstrate, by their number and range, the impracticality of characterizing it—hence one of its titles, the Ineffable.

Being the fundamental factor, or first principle, it can be said to be the pre-existing condition in which (or out of which) all existent things arise. While all things derive their existence as a corollary of it, it—uniquely—is self-existent.

Yet, without manifestations of it, it in and of itself represents no thing, or nothing. Thus, it is also described as Emptiness, or the Void. Put another way, without beings to attest that it exists, it would not be known as existent.

Because it is known as self-existent, it is generally recognized to be without beginning or ending. What has been called the Infinite or the Totality supercedes any limitations in either space or time; both space and time conceivably have a beginning and ending. The Totality, on the other hand, is said to be unbounded, illimitable, immeasurable in space, unlimited by time.

That which has no beginning or ending has no borders, restraints or restrictions. All *forms* have a limitation in time or space. That which is perfectly illimitable would be formless.

The important point, which spiritual teachings emphasize, is that a ubiquitous actuality that is entirely unrestrained in space or time would be irresistibly present—everywhere, at all times.

This would mean that, having no barrier to its presence at any point ever in any time or any place, it would not only have surrounded every thing or form which ever existed, it would (at any and every moment) penetrate, permeate and saturate every entity which has been, is, or will be.

In other words, it is understood to be the essence of all of actuality—in fact, the *essential* be-ing of all that is.

It is generally considered to be the ground or source of being. All things or forms arise within it, exist within it (or we could say, *as* it), and eventually return to this immutable condition.

The spiritual teachers emphasize that all forms (whether material or immaterial) are impermanent, transient. But *that* eternal and infinite presence in which all existent things arise and subside is not itself impermanent.

The impermanent forms are called *relative*, in that they are dependent upon changing conditions, within time and space. That which all else is dependent upon, and which is not itself subject to change, they call the *Absolute* (the word actually means "not relative;" it also means "without limitation." All of the myriad names or titles for the ultimate actuality are summed up in that word, which spiritual texts have utilized universally.)

18

But the important point, which is often overlooked, is that the relative and the Absolute are not two different, or separate, actualities. There is only One actuality, though we might refer to it in its manifested *appearance* as any particular (or general) relative *form*; or, alternately, we might consider its essential nature as the *omnipresent* being-ness in which each thing has *Absolute* expression. The two aspects cannot in any way be considered to be apart from each other: the relative is within the Absolute, at the same time that the Absolute is within the relative. This, then, explains the paradoxes elaborated by the teachings and their teachers. Complete clarity regarding the paradoxical nature of ultimate reality is known as enlightenment, realization, or awakening.

Another name for enlightenment is nondual awareness, or Absolute awareness. It is also described as the transcendence of the dualistic perspective.

The rishis say that our underlying condition, or true nature, is the formless presence or being-ness that is the essential element in (or of) every form. When you go to sleep at night, there are several times (scientists confirm) when you go into such a deep sleep that "pure awareness" is all that is present. There is some sort of vital presence, because if someone were to pinch you, or yell "Fire!," you'd wake up.

But in this condition of deep sleep, there is no sense of being some particular "person," no concepts, no conception of "others"—in fact, no perception of a world, or even of a universe. There is simply empty awareness.

When we wake out of sleep, there are bodily needs and conscious attention is directed toward attending to the needs of the physical organism. As a consequence, we subjectively operate in the material surroundings, from the standpoint of relative considerations and conceptual relationships.

In other words, although in deep sleep we do not conceive of any individuated selves, in the waking state we think in terms of "my self" and "other selves." It is this "relative" perspective which is referred to as *duality*.

In the state of deep sleep, where there is no awareness of even one "thing," that empty condition is what is indicative of *nonduality*. The rishis say that it is out of this formless, nondual awareness that the separative, dualistic thoughts (which we utilize in the waking state) are formed and consciously perceived.

The nature of the thinking process is that it is divisive. We think in the form of words, which are themselves separative, and our thinking process entails comparison and selection: choices upon which to act.

This process has practical value, in the material world, in terms of deciding (and pursuing) our bodily needs. However, our divisive, or dualistic, thought patterns lead us into conflict: me versus you; us/them; friend/enemy; and so on.

It particularly leads to the conclusion that "I" and some "other" thing, or reality, are separate from each other: principally, that I and God (or Ultimate Reality) are two different things. The idea then becomes to seek some sort of "union" with God, or the Absolute.

The rishis say that the formless awareness, which is at your core, is a manifestation of the Absolute. It is the ground of being for your every thought, conception or conclusion—and this even *includes* your thoughts or feelings of separativeness.

This is why they say in the scriptures "*You* are not the Doer." They say that every thought, word or action—whether positive or negative—arises from the nondual Essence.

But, again, it would be a mistake to think of the formless Absolute as in any way apart from any of the relative forms. As the Bhagavad Gita makes clear, both the killer and the killed are forms of That (the Ultimate Reality) in its expression.

20

Since you and the Absolute cannot in any way be apart or separate, when this truth is clearly and thoroughly realized it is known as enlightenment. It is also called Self-realization. (Self is another appellation for the Absolute, the point being that it is *your* "self" that is recognized to be the limitless actuality.)

One of the questions that the spiritual literature responds to is, what is the affect of Self-realization, or Absolute awareness, on one's life.

In the first place, when the *seeking* for "union," or the end of fragmentation, is concluded; the finder of ultimate Truth, or the enlightened one, is called a *jnani* (pr: nyaani), which means knower, or seer.

For this seer, the multitudinous forms which compose the relative world have not disappeared. These continue to be recognized, but are now viewed differently. In other words, one continues to access relative reality as it has been utilized to serve the organism's needs. But now there's an additional dimension which hadn't been incorporated before, nondual awareness concerning the nature of reality.

And once this awareness is clearly present, it does not dissipate. It's akin to the discovery that a person can experience with an optical illusion: once the extra dimension has been clearly apprehended, it can continually be perceived from that point on.

Here's how the jnani explains what is continuously seen. Every form (whether material or immaterial) is limited to a beginning and an ending; all are changeable, impermanent, transient. The infinite Presence in which all forms arise and subside is not limited by beginning or ending: it is the only actuality which is permanent and immutable. So the sage says that the only thing which has lasting reality is the ground of Being; all which appears from and returns to It is

21

"unreal," by comparison. This is why the rishis state that the world is a dream or an illusion: when we close our eyes for the last time, every *thing* will utterly disappear—in the same way that the world, in our dreams, vanishes in the waking state.

Beyond, then, the seer "seeing through" the relative *appearances* and perceiving fundamentally the limitless Essence at their core—and therefore having ended his notion that the Essence eludes him—there is an even more profound consequence.

Once this comprehension is in place, this finder cannot help but recognize that the very essence of his own (impermanent) form is this unbounded Presence which itself is beyond birth or death. This is what the Vedas mean when they state *tat tvam asi*: That thou art. The jnani senses completely that no matter what he thinks, says or does—*and* no matter what anyone *else* thinks, says or does—it is "That, doing what it does."

This is the basic element of the life-changing development known as Self-realization, or awakening. Once this has become profoundly transparent—the ultimate truth that "all that *is*, is essentially That"—then *this* is consequently recognized: "All that is being done is That doing what it does."

In other words, what had previously been (prior to awakening) a *self*-centered fixation has now become a focused awareness of the Self. And this is not an awareness, once present, that needs to be "maintained." Once nondual clarity is perceived, it becomes as customary as our dualistic perspective had previously been. There are no practices or disciplines necessary to sustain it.

One development the Self-realized will likely notice is a change in values. The concern for "me," "my," and "mine"

22

is relinquished. One becomes an objective, impartial witness to developments which unfold—both to and around the seer. And, as a result of the dispassioned nonattachment which ensues, one begins to notice changes in one's behavior. This is likely to be of the characterization of "action without concern for outcome," as contrasted to what one had previously experienced as self-serving, or exploitative, reactions.

There will also likely be noticed the freeing up of creative energy, which had previously been invested in creating, maintaining and defending a self-image, or ego.

The most noticeable development, particularly to other observers, will probably be recognized as the diminution of conflict, both inward and outward. This results in the oft-cited peace and freedom which enlightenment entails.

In realizing the unbroken, seamless wholeness and interconnection of all that is, the jnani transcends the divisive "pairs of opposites" which duality represents. He no longer thinks in terms of such polarities as "positive/negative," "better/worse," "right/wrong," "good/bad," and so forth. He ceases to qualify phenomena, which are witnessed in awareness, by attaching names or labels—such as "pride," "envy," "anger," ad infinitum. He finds himself being impartially "present with whatever is present."

The primary dualistic spectrum which he has disassociated with is that of "should be" and "should not be." Whatever is noticed on the screen of consciousness as an existent fact, or 'what is,' is not supposed by him that it ought to be something other than what it is. He transcends the notion that any particular thing which is noticed—internally or externally—should *instead* be some *other* thing which it, in actuality, is not.

Reality is not subject to our desires, as to how it *ought* to unfold; or, as to how it is *already* manifesting in the present moment. To have ideas, or expectations, about what a particular situation or condition *could* instead be, or *not* be, is merely pointless mentation. It is such ideas which become ideals (for our own behavior and that of others), leading to a primary cause of inner and outer conflict.

So, the jnani witnesses whatever phenomena happens to be presently occurring (regarding himself or the world) without categorizing it as "good" or "bad," or having an attachment to a particular outcome. This is what the spiritual literature calls "*choiceless* awareness."

It is this non-judgmental disposition which allows the jnani to cease self-critique (as well as the judgmental assessment of others). While he witnesses each thought which appears in consciousness, he does not conclude that any particular thought is more, or less, preferential than any other. Therefore, there is not anything which appears on the screen of consciousness which perturbs him. In particular, he has no notion that he ought to *be* any way other than the way he is at the moment. In other words, there are no ideas concerning "self-improvement."

With ideals, opinions, expectations, beliefs, fixations, et cetera, laid aside, his is an "empty mind;" he utilizes discursive cognition where it is practical, but otherwise his attention is focused on what's immediately present. In witnessing, his is an unbroken meditation, or contemplation. His tendency is to be spontaneous, un-self-conscious, alert but relaxed.

(For a sense of how the nondual insight is experienced in the lives of various people, you might like to read my book *Living Nonduality*, which contains 238 monographs on various aspects of Self-realization. You can also visit www.livingnonduality.org.)

Using the English translation by Nityaswarupananda, let's now see how the nondual teachings are expressed in the Ashtavakra Gita.

Our thought process utilizes designated words and pictured images. Each word, or image, is a particular, separate form. Thought has a practical value, in that it facilitates the breaking up of a panoramic reality so that we can manipulate the individual "pieces" to accomplish our necessary tasks. The intrinsic nature of thought, however, is divisive. We may, where needed, "unite" some of the pieces, but the pieces were initially of our own creation.

So, each name that we give to something (whether material or immaterial) establishes it, in our thinking, as a separate form or entity. If we say that something is "soft," that means that it is "not hard": so the two definitions, or concepts or ideas, arise mutually; soft as opposed to hard. If we say there is "one thing," this suggests that there could be more (or less) than one thing: two things, for example. So when we identify "one," the potentiality of "two or more" (or, "less than one") *gives* "one" its conceptual form.

The thought process which creates named forms can also dissolve them. Each form is within the boundary of its definition; definitions can change, be enlarged, be deconstructed. In fact, everything which fits within the boundary of its name is subject to change; appearance and disappearance. My "house," as a form, is impermanent: it was created in time, and will be destroyed in time. My "body" is a similar form; it has made an appearance in time and will disappear in time. Even something immaterial, such as my memories, have a beginning and will have an ending.

So, one point that the Ashtavakra Gita establishes is that every *thing*, which we can conceive of, has taken form in our thoughts, and will at some time cease to exist. And, while existent, we think in terms of forms as separate from each other: e.g., my "body" and the "universe." When we perceive such pluralistic forms, this is known as duality, and the forms are said to be "relative" to each other.

The Ashtavakra Gita makes more than two dozen references to our ingrained habit of thinking in dualistic, or relative, terms. For example (chapter-verse): praise or blame 3-10; gain versus loss 15-11; near and far, or in and out 19-6; pleasure versus pain 3-14; virtue and vice 4-3; heaven or hell 18-80; happy versus angry 8-1 and 8-2; man or woman 17-15; life and death 17-6. Dualistic divisiveness also applies to "triads," such as knower, knowing and known 2-15.

A particularly troublesome dualistic pair is our notion that we need to either "accept" or "reject" some particular state, or reality, that we find ourselves in (8-4; one of at least 10 mentions).

So, in comprehending the divisiveness of the dualistic perspective, the enlightened have transcended the conception of separative forms. The Gita instructs:

26

Do not find any duality. The wise do not see "this" and "that," they do not perceive the "relative". Completely give up distinctions—the "world" of the relative is transcended by the wise. Free from the pairs of opposites (such as better-worse), the sage sees the same everywhere—his perception is nondual. Duality is the root of misery.

Because reality is an unbroken, indivisible whole—before thought parses it into a myriad of conceived forms—the *initial* reality is considered, by the enlightened, to be the truth of actuality. The conception of dualistic, and impermanent, forms is thereby described as an illusion (or unreal, like a dream), merely the product of our selective and diversive thought process.

> **The wise are free of discriminatory imaginings and know all as mere "idea." They look upon objects and conditions as a dream. With the dawning of enlightened knowledge, all delusion becomes like a dream.**

> **All this time, Janaka said about his prior state upon his awakening, I have been duped by illusion: through illusion, ultimate reality appears as if it were confined to the "world." Worlds however are produced with the rising of the differentiating mind.**

The world disappears with the knowledge of undivided reality.

All this is the product of illusion, and nothing exists as "objects" in an undivided reality. The "universe" itself is a figment of imagination. The universe, even though it seems present to the senses, is unreal. With the calming of the wind of the mind creating forms, the universe meets destruction (as a defined object). The universe does not in reality exist. This manifold universe is nothing...nothing exists.

The wise one therefore is unattached to the objects of this world. Attachment to the objects of illusory perception arises from ignorance of undivided reality. Be intent on complete indifference to the world; realizing this universe as mere illusion, how can one fear even "death"?

Forms—having a beginning and an ending, thus impermanent—are said to arise and subside like waves. The undivided primal reality—*through which* the forms arise, appear as objects, and then subside—is not itself merely another of the impermanent forms. Put another way, the forms are a manifestation of a condition, or presence, which is not itself limited to a beginning and ending: it would be said to be infinite in space, and eternal in time.

And being without beginning and ending, it would be absolutely unlimited—devoid of borders, boundaries, restrictions or restraints of any sort. It would not, then, be any kind of entity: it would be formless.

And, whereas the forms (which appear within its unlimited presence) are impermanent, the infinite and eternal formless condition would be the only reality which *is* permanent.

Also, while the forms change—come and go—the formless presence is (being beyond the limitations of time and place) forever unchanging.

Additionally, being the source (or "ground") of all that "exists"—all this is manifested—it would be said to be the "nothingness" out of which "something-ness" appears; formlesseness is sometimes described as "emptiness," or the void. But: although "empty," all *things* are said to be "within" it—because every *thing* is limited, while formlessness is infinite.

So, the ground of being, which itself is empty (or void) of "thingness," does not stand as even "one thing" (being really "no-thing"), much less "two"—or additional—things. Therefore, this formless condition is said to be the epitome of nonduality.

The sages, then, when they speak of transcending duality through a radical shift in awareness, or perspective, are speaking of recognizing the formless ground of being as the ultimate reality, and all the apparent objects (within the formless) as insubstantial creations with no independent reality. Chapter 1, verse18: **Know that which has form to be unreal, and the formless to be permanent.**

There is, however, a confusing issue which needs to be pointed out. Because all things are said to exist within the void of formlessness, all things are sometimes said to be "one," to be subject to the same mutual reality. And since the things are not *outside of*, or apart from, the infinite presence they exist within, it is sometimes depicted that the formless—*including* all that is within it—is One. So, despite the primary description of formlessness as no-thing, it sometimes is *also* alluded to as One, or "one, without a second"—meaning to say, a nondualistic *one*.

While the preceding teachings of the enlightened sage are, sometimes, difficult enough to grasp, there is an aspect of the formless reality which is crucial to Self-realization, but best comprehended in the context of the discussion given so far.

The ultimate reality (or ground of Being), from which all *things* arise and to which all return, is formless and boundless, and thus is unconfined or unrestricted in either space or time. Hence it is infinite and eternal, not ever absent from any moment of time nor point in space. Therefore, it is the condition, or medium, in which all forms appear.

Being ever-present everywhere, it surrounds every existent form. But, being free of any hindrance or limitation, it also—simultaneously—penetrates, pervades and saturates every conceivable form. As the Vedas state, *"Nowhere is it not."* So, this indivisible actuality is not only the source of every thing, but also the deepest identity (or essence) of all that has taken appearance through it.

This element of the nondual teachings is profoundly important for Self-realization. It is the basis of the foundational insight that the infinite and eternal Being, or presence, not only is inescapably the subject of every one of your senses, but is the inward "You" who is aware and conscious of what is sensed. *And* the ultimate Beingness is not only your underlying identity (or "true nature"), but that of every other form or thing which exists.

In other words, the entire universe can said to be It (or That, as the ultimate reality is also termed). And this does not mean that each *thing* is a "part" of it; the indivisible formlessness (or Totality), being ubiquitous, does not admit of any partitions, divisions or parts.

As the same all-pervading air is *inside* and *outside* a jar, even so the Eternal all-pervasive exists in all things—It in all, and all in It. The universe is permeated by It through and through. It exists inside and outside this body. The universe, emanating from It, is not different from It and this universe, duly considered, is nothing but It. The universe, which has emanated from It, will dissolve into It.

Spiritual literature, throughout the ages, has utilized a variety of terms or names to allude to the ultimate reality: Brahman, Tao, God, Being, Omnipresence, That, It—just to name a few. The Ashtavakra Gita itself uses at least a half dozen of such terms. Commonly, the word *Self* is employed to indicate the "real" self, the essence of what everyone (or everything) ultimately is. In religious texts, the term might be Divine, Sacred or Holy, even Spirit. One word, though, can be found in every religious or spiritual tradition: Absolute. It means "not relative," but it is also defined as "without limitation." To make matters simple, it will be used here, in most cases.

The Gita, of course, has much to say about the Absolute— at least two dozen references, employing various of the alternate names. Since both Janaka and Ashtavakra are speaking as the Self-realized, who are fully conscious of being That, they sometimes speak *as* the Absolute. So, by saying "me" or "I" (or "you," to each other), they are speaking from the Absolute "point of view" (non-relative, or nondual).

From the enlightened standpoint (sometimes called Absolute awareness), the Self is all-inclusive; it not only encompasses all things, but embodies all things. For those for whom this is understood, paradoxical sayings are clarified.

However, any attempt to describe the "empty" formlessness is a challenge to our *thinking* process, since every *word* is itself a form.

Since even consciousness has the Absolute as its source, the term Consciousness is sometimes also an alternate.

By now, you'll recognize some the descriptions (and varied titles) of the Absolute:

The Self is absolute.

The Self is all-pervading—through illusion, it appears of the world.

The Self neither comes nor goes.

The Self is not an object of perception.

The Self is One, without a second.

That *in* which the universe appears.

That which is *beyond* all objects.

The One *only* was, is and will be.

The ever Undifferentiated.

Free from limitation.

Pervades this universe, and this universe exists in It.

Unchanging, *I* neither increase nor decrease.

I am really Consciousness itself.

I am indeed in all beings, and all beings are in Me.

For the wise one, there is Nothing whatsoever.

Probably the most difficult realization for the seeker of the Absolute to grasp is that the seeker *is* the sought. As the Vedas have said, "The observer *is* the observed." In other words, that person which is seeing is of the very same essence as anything which can be seen.

"That (the Absolute)," the Vedas state, "*thou* art." With that deep-seated recognition, the sense or idea of being a "separate" individual—a "self"—falls away. It is this very identification as a particular self—our I-thought—which is the root of our perception of division, the source of conflict with "others" and consequent suffering for every "person."

> **The wise one lives without the feeling of I-ness or mine-ness. What is this I, or what is "mine"? Be devoid of the feeling of mine-ness and I-ness, knowing for certain that Nothing is—in Me, individual selves rise and disappear.**

This aspect of the nondual teachings—that there is, in actuality, no such independent being as an I—leads to a Vedic phrase that some "persons" have difficulty with: "You are not the doer."

The Doer of all that is done, ultimately, is the Absolute. And given the circumstance that you and the Absolute are "not two," then in that sense it could be said that you *are* the doer (of deeds)—*as* the Absolute, "you" are doing what is done (by that body which you may think of as "you").

The point of the saying is that if you *do* identify your self as the *body*—rather than as the Self that is transcendent of all forms—then you need to recognize that it is not that (small) self which is the ubiquitous Actor in every action. What others see as "your" actions (such as even speaking or thinking), you—knowing you are That—regard as the actions of Beingness.

> **Egoism says "I am the doer." The sage says, I am not the body, nor is the body "mine." I am Absoluteness. He who has an egotistic feeling and considers even the body his own, suffers misery. The man of knowledge does not "act," though "he" may be acting. One who says "this" is done by the *body*, but not by "me"—such a one, even though acting, does not act.**

With the (illusive) supposition of being a separate I, an "individual," dissolved, along with the recognition that whatever is manifest (even one's thought, speech and actions) is That doing what it does, the Self-realized is free of the notion and pursuit of "self"-improvement. The Absolute, which he knows himself to be, can be neither "increased nor decreased," nor does the sage think in (dualistic) terms such as "better" or "worse."

> **Give up self-modification. The sage says no "good" or "evil" accrues to me. One who knows turns away from what is attained and not attained. Do not disturb your mind with affirmation and negation.**

The Self-realized recognizes that the Absolute is not something that is merely far out in space, or far away in time. Being omni-present—as every spiritual and religious tradition declares—it must of necessity be as immediate to us as is our every heartbeat, our every breath. Therefore, there is nowhere that we need to go, and nothing that we need to do, in order to be "in contact" with the Absolute. In fact, the

Absolute is inescapable! Enlightenment, or Self-realization, is simply a matter of clearly apprehending this truth.

Thus, any type of activity we engage with the notion that it will bring one "closer" to the Absolute, or Self, is actually a diversion and distraction *away* from That which is always present as the essential nature of all which exists. The Absolute cannot help but be *here now*, wherever and whenever "here and now" are to you.

The Ashtavakra Gita makes more than two dozen references to point out that it is self-interested desire which is at the root of so-called spiritual practices (what in Buddhism is called a "gaining" idea). The notion is that the individual practitioner will *become* One, through diligent effort: this is ignor-ance of the truth that there is already nothing *but* One.

For example, rather than attempting to "control the mind," the sage comprehends that the mind is merely another manifestation, or expression of the Absolute; the sage is simply consciously witnessing whatever appears on the screen of awareness. *And* since the sage and the Self are not two, it is essentially the Self which is the real seer.

> **You are the One seer of all: unattached, formless and witness of all you are. The Self is witness, all-pervading, One, actionless, desireless. Know the Self as the witness of all, and Consciousness itself—you are not the body, nor is the body yours, nor are you the doer. You are the eternal Witness, and free.**

Being One already, any desire to *become* One by "practicing" reveals a dualistic premise: I am "me," and the Self is "not-me," so these two things could be brought together at some time or place in the future. The longest Ashtavakra Gita chapter (18) devotes many versus to this error.

Because he *desires* to *become* It, the *seeker* does *not* attain. Betaking yourself to firm non-attachment, go beyond desire. Glorious is he who is free from all desires, and is the embodiment of the Infinite which is his own nature.

The sage is without motive. The sage says meditation, renunciation of the objects of the mind are distractions to Me. The wise man, whose delight is in the Self and whose mind is calm, has no desire for renouncing anything, nor does he feel any loss anywhere. The phenomenal world has neither to be renounced nor accepted.

The sage is not distracted even in "distraction," is not meditative even in meditation—where is meditation of That, for the one who is beyond the world of desires? Where is "control of mind" for the deluded one who strives for it?

The seeker does not attain liberation through activity by way of repeated practice. The ignorant constantly take to the practice of concentration and control of the mind. The frightened ones seek for the attainment of control and concentration. Completely give up even concentration, and *hold* nothing in your mind: you are verily the Self, and therefore free.

Freedom of action (or inaction) and peace of mind are important aspects of what Self-realization provides—particularly freedom from the conflicts (outer or inner) that the dualistic perspective generates; such as "us" versus "them," and "me" separated from "God."

> **The one who knows That for certain becomes free from the conflict of thought, and peaceful. The mind is never "yours": you are free from conflict.**

> **Rules of conduct, renunciation, and restraint—what are they to one who is of the nature of That? Who can prohibit that one, who has known this entire universe to be the Self alone, from living as he pleases? Glorious is the life of the wise one who is free of expectation, free from all attachments, free from desire for the objects of the senses, and free from care even for his own body. Having Absolute knowledge, now do as you please.**

Buddha was said, in the post-Vedic period, to have often spoken about suffering. But the Pali word that is translated as *suffering* might best be translated as *discontent*.

Buddha pointed out there was a cause underlying suffering: that at the *root* of suffering is dis-satisfaction— disagreement with *what is*. The sage does not argue with what the Absolute has disposed to do, and thus is placid, tranquil and unconflicted. As "praise" and "blame" are the same to him, "this" eventuality rather than "that" eventuality are of no concern either. This serene stillness is what is often referred to as "bliss," in the spiritual literature. The long 18th chapter of the Ashtavakra has much to say about the sage's perceptive equanimity.

> **Contentment ever dwells in the heart of the wise one who lives with whatever comes to him.**
>
> **The liberated one who has no desire is contented, and indifferent to everything**
>
> **The desireless one is contented, and the same in "happiness" and "misery."**

The wise one is contented under all conditions.

One who is desireless, whose "sorrow" is destroyed, is contented with repose in the Self.

The wise one has attained repose. He is reposing on the foundation of his own Being.

Blessed indeed is that knower of Self, who is the same in all conditions.

There is no "joy" or "sorrow" for one who has transcended worldly existence: ever with a serene mind he lives.

He is not at all perturbed, even when ridiculed.

He does not feel "elated," abiding in that nondual state.

The tranquil-minded one remains the same in any condition.

The wise one knows the Truth and is ever of tranquil mind. Rare is the one who is thus calm.

A wise man becomes quiet by realizing that all this existence is transient, unsubstantial.

Equanimous in practical life as well, the wise one sits happily.

He who gains a knowledge of the true nature of Consciousness by means of complete indifference to the world, equanimity, is he not really a spiritual guide?

The one who has known for certain that all this world is the product of illusion, and that nothing exists, naturally enjoys peace.

You are equanimous in "misery" and "happiness," hope and despair, and life and death.

By now, it should be clear that the Self-realized one lives a wholly different life than the typical person. The Ashtavakra Gita devotes the majority of its content to describing this perspective of the enlightened one, with Ashtavakra speaking from his own experience and Janaka speaking from what is being revealed to him, as now also one of the Self-realized. Since there are more than five dozen such referential statements, they can be gathered into loose subjective groups.

To comprehend the teachings of the Self-realized, you need to be firmly grounded in the element of "indivisibility" which nonduality represents, as distinct from the "individuality" of *things* which duality conceives. You also need to recognize that while there *appear* to be independent, relative "things," not *any* thing is independent of the indivisible Absolute. "Seeing through" this appearance is Self-realization. And what is seen—though it sounds paradoxical—is no-thing. But there is no contradiction: from the standpoint of nondual realization, both the thingness and nothingness are an interdependent actuality ("suchness," in Buddhism).

"Parts" have no significance for the one who has transcended such dual notions as "this is" and "this is not." What are named objects to me who am ever devoid of the

45

sense of duality? What would he who has transcended all concepts meditate on when he sees no "second"? What is the "world"... to me who am nondual in my nature?

The man of wisdom is free from the pairs of opposites; giving up thoughts of "loss" and "elation," I live happily. The sage knows not the conflict of "good" and "evil"; he abides in the state of Absoluteness.

I am indivisible, and established in Self; he has gained the fruit of Knowledge who, contented, ever enjoys being alone.

The desireless one is contented, and the same in "happiness" and "misery." Glorious is the life of the wise one who is free from expectation—such a one turns away from what is "attained" and "not attained." Easily refrain from "accepting" or "rejecting" anything.

One who knows for certain that this manifold universe is nothing becomes desireless, and finds peace.

There are about three dozen of the gita's verses which attempt to describe what can be said of the discovery of Self-realization in general, as well as in particular. This sums up, in a practical way, the teachings.

A wise person will gain enlightenment even by instruction that is casually imparted.

Salutation to That with the dawning of the Knowledge of which all delusion disappears like a dream.

No sooner is the Self apprehended, with the cessation of illusion, than they—with their vision unobstructed—live with their sorrows dispelled.

Knowing for certain that one's self is That, "existence" and "nonexistence" are figments.

He is free from attachment to all objects. Who has realized the Truth is devoid of all attachment.

One without attachment is free from sorrow.

The knower of Truth is never miserable; by nonattachment is attained constant joy of the realization of the Self.

One becomes peaceful, with all his desires set at rest within; and is not attached to anything whatsoever.

An indescribable state is attained by the sage who is free from the divergent display of the mind, and from delusion, dream.

The liberated person is always found abiding in Self. "I am Self": constantly aware in this way, I am abiding in the Absolute.

The nature of the Self is absolute, effortless; verily neither far away nor "attained."

He has become silent by knowing for certain all as Self.

The liberated one rests in the Self under all conditions; is the same everywhere; does not reflect on what he "has" or "has not" done.

You are the Self.

I have realized the supreme Self, who is the Witness; I feel no anxiety for emancipation (seeking has ended).

He is free from doubts and has his mind absorbed in the Self.

The wise one becomes happy merely by ascertaining the Truth.

Know That to be one; and enter into the state of dissolution. The man of Knowledge is devoid of divisive thought, and devoid of the sense of ego. Wherefrom will there be egotism for thee who art One? When there is no "I," there is liberation.

His nature is free from conditions: acting as he pleases, the wise one is not affected by "honor" or "dishonor." He moves about at his own pleasure, and can only be understood by those Self-realized like him. Only those like him understand his liberated state.

Realizing the *Self* in all—and *all* in the Self—and free from egoism, and the sense of "mine," he is happy.

The man of Knowledge lives happily on whatever subsistence comes as a matter of course. Where is even fear, for me who abides in Self?

Praised, he does not feel pleased; and blamed, he does not get annoyed: he neither rejoices in life, nor fears death.

For me, who am reposing in Self, there is no need of talking about the "end of life." Reposing on the foundation of his own Being...he cares not whether his body dies. He is not perturbed at the sight of approaching death. Let the body go, even today: where is there any increase or decrease in You?

This knowledge of the Truth is shunned by those who want to enjoy the "world."

Like the numerous discourses of spiritual teachings called *upanishads* or *gitas* recorded during India's Vedic period, there are many texts called *sutras* recorded after Buddha's lifetime. Often cited are the Heart Sutra, the Lotus Sutra and the Diamond Sutra. The latter is the sutra which Hui Neng, the Sixth Chinese Patriarch, is said to have overheard someone reciting, which led to his enlightenment; he later delivered a commentary on this sutra, in his capacity as a Zen master.

Of its many translations into English, a 2001 edition—*The Diamond Sutra: The Perfection of Wisdom*, by the translator who uses the name Red Pine—presents the sutra in 27 pages (and then an interpretation of the verses for another four hundred pages).

In the Translator's Preface, he suggests that the Buddha spoke on this sutra's subject matter circa 400 B.C., and emphasized "*emptiness* is the true nature of reality."

In a format similar to king Janaka asking pertinent questions of the sage Ashtavakra, in the Ashtavakra Gita, this sutra is comprised of questions posed to Buddha by a "venerable" disciple, Subhuti. And in the same way that it developed that Janaka spoke with the same enlightened perspective as his guru Ashtavakra, in rhetorical questions which Buddha puts to his seasoned disciple Subhuti, the responses given by *either* of them are intended to enunciate the enlightenment teachings.

There is a consistent thread which runs throughout the (thirty-two sectioned) exchanges between Buddha and Subhuti. Early on, Buddha states that those who "gain perfect clarity of mind" (enlightenment), "do not create the perception of a *self.* Nor do they create the perception of a *being,* a *life*..."

Even Buddha, prior to his enlightenment, had "created a self." We all do; we are conditioned into the perspective of "self"-existence, right from infancy. The prince Gautama was no exception. But he, in his spiritual awakening, *transcended* the perspective of "self" identity.

But this self-identity is normally a continuous one in our thoughts. In the enlightened sage's thoughts, from moment to moment, he (or she) does not "create"—or re-create— this erroneous perception. In other words, he is "empty" of such—and similar—false perceptions, and this results in "perfect clarity of mind."

Throughout the Sutra, the implied subject is "dharma"; while this word can have multiple meanings, here it means principally *reality.* The "self" would be said to be empty of dharma, inasmuch as it has no sustainable reality.

In fact, all "things," every *thing,* is similarly and equally empty of reality, because *dharma* is transcendent of "thingnesss"; by its nature, it is undifferentiated. So, that which dharma transcends—all things—are "unreal"; only the transcendent dharma has (is) reality.

Therefore, even Buddha is unreal, to the extent that he is viewed as some *thing;* or, in particular, as a "self." Likewise he would not, either, be a "being," as an entity; consequently, it could not be said that he had a "life."

The emptiness of things applies to *conceived* things, as well as substantial or *material* things. The (insubstantial) "self" is merely the prime example. To even say that there is such a thing as "existence," on the one hand, *or* "nonexistence," is to make a differentiation which has no reality from the standpoint of dharma.

Thus, Buddha says, in this Sutra, "in the dharma (reality) realized, taught and reflected on" by him (the Tathagata), "there is nothing true and nothing false." He cannot claim any such *thing*.

So, he quizzes his disciple: "Subhuti, if someone should claim the Tathagata speaks of a view of a self, or that the Tathagata speaks of a view of a being, a view of a life, or a view of a soul, Subhuti, would such a claim be true?" Subhuti said, "No, indeed, Bhagavan."

With this background, we can follow the thread of nondual instruction through section after section.

Where there is no such thing as a self, there is no self which perceives a "world." The Buddha said, "Subhuti, if any bodhisattva should thus claim, 'I shall bring about the transformation of a world,' such a claim would be untrue." Subhuti acknowledges that he "dwells no where at all." After all, "buddhas and bhagavans are free of *all* perceptions"; that would include any such conception as a "world."

"The Buddha said...Neither can someone who creates the perception of a life [his or others'], or even the perception of a soul [or afterlife], be called a bodhisattva." He emphasizes, "No beginning [and thus no finite ending], Subhuti, is the highest truth.... And thus does the Tathagata say 'all dharmas have no self, all dharmas have no life, no individuality, and no soul'.... Subhuti, this dharma teaching cannot be heard by (those) who mistakenly perceive a self..."

Where there is no self, there is no thinker who creates differentiated perceptions, or thoughts. "Subhuti, a past thought cannot be found. A future thought cannot be found. Nor can a present thought be found."

"Subhuti," said Buddha, "undifferentiated is this dharma, in which nothing (no thing) is differentiated."

The Buddha said, "Subhuti, what do you think? Does it occur to the Tathagata: 'I teach a dharma'?"

Subhuti replied, "No, indeed, Bhagavan. It does not occur to the Tathagata: 'I teach a dharma.'"

The Buddha said, "Subhuti, if someone should claim, 'the Tathagata teaches a dharma,' such a claim would be untrue. Such a view of *me*, Subhuti, would be a *misconception*."

"Subhuti, what do you think? Does it occur to the Tathagata: 'I rescue beings?' Surely, Subhuti, you should hold no such view. And why not? Subhuti, the *being* does *not exist* who is rescued by the Tathagata. Subhuti, if any being were rescued by the Tathagata, the Tathagata would be attached to a *self*. He would be attached to a being, attached to a life..."

"Furthermore, Subhuti, if anyone should claim that the Tathagata goes or comes or stands or sits or lies on a bed, Subhuti, they do not understand the meaning of my words. And why not? Subhuti, those who are called 'tathagatas' do not go anywhere, nor do they come from anywhere. Thus are they called 'tathagata, fully-enlightened ones.'"

On that occasion the Buddha then spoke this:

> Who looks for me in form,
> who seeks me in a voice,
> indulges in wasted effort;
> such people see me not.

And he said, as "an illusion…a bubble, a dream…view all 'created' *things* like this."

Subhuti comprehended: "Bhagavan, if a *universe* existed, attachment to an *entity* would exist."

The Buddha said…"Foolish people, though, *are* attached."

He advised that each discover "the self-less, birthless nature" of reality; renounce "self-existence *every day*"; "and master this entire teaching, and explain it in *detail* to others. For in that place, Subhuti, dwells a teacher or one who represents the guru of wisdom."

And Subhuti states: "Sages arise from what is *uncreated*."

One of the briefest of the Upanishads is also one of the most highly regarded among spiritual masters. Ramana Maharshi sometimes referenced it.

The Mandukya Upanishad: An Exposition is one among a number of English renditions of this classic nondual text (by Swami Krishnananda, who follows its presentation with 130 pages of discussion).

Only about a dozen paragraphs in all, the Mandukya Upanishad focuses on what is called *prajna* in Sanskrit; while *prajna* is often translated as one word, "wisdom," it more closely means "knowing Reality." In other words, recognizing that the ever-present Self is actually the self of our perception, or awareness. As the Upanishad states, "the Self; *this* is to be realized." Self-realization is another word for enlightenment, or Absolute (nondual) awareness.

The Upanishad compares this realized waking state to the condition all of us experience in our deepest sleep: "one asleep neither desires anything, nor beholds any dream: that is deep sleep. In this field of dreamless sleep, one becomes undivided, an undifferentiated mass of consciousness..." This "empty" condition, it indicates, is prajna; the self at one with the Self, or Reality.

And it describes this "nondual" ground of being, or "Source of All" as "without a second." That is, there is not anything besides, beyond, apart or outside of the One: "This is the *beginning* and *end* of all beings." Its Absolute, incomparable nature is depicted as "invisible, ineffable, intangible, devoid of characteristics, inconceivable, undefinable, its sole essence being the consciousness of its own Self; the coming to rest of all *relative* existence…"

The Mandukya Upanishad concludes, "He who knows thus (Reality), merges the self in the Self."

Fast forward across the centuries, from the writing of the Ashtavakra Gita, the Diamond Sutra, and Mandukya Upanishad, to the first half of the twentieth century and to a sage who lived the nondual teachings and expounded them.

As a sixteen-year-old schoolboy in south India, Ramana Maharshi (an honorific name bestowed on him in later years), experienced a spontaneous nondual realization. He left home and traveled to a south Indian mountain, Arunachala, where enlightened sages traditionally tended to gather. Living the life of a renunicate, spiritual seekers were so attracted by the purity of his dedication that an ashram was built for him where he resided uninterrupted for about the last 30 years of his life; the ashram still exists there. He died (of cancer) in 1950, at age 71.

Particularly during his years at the ashram, hundreds of seekers engaged Ramana in discussions concerning various aspects of Self-realization. During about four years, in the late 1930's, a disciple kept a written record of the daily dialogues which Ramana then perused to assure the accuracy of its nondual teachings. Some 650 of these discussions, of varying lengths, were published in 1955, titled *Talks with Sri Ramana Maharshi*; by the year 2000, it was already in its tenth reprint. The major source for Ramana's complete teachings, its 683 pages include a 24-page index, an 8-page bibliography of other Ramana sources, and a 10-page glossary for any Sanskrit references.

Ramana sometimes quotes the Ashtavakra Gita, in *Talks*. And, like the Gita, the nondual precepts are expounded somewhat randomly in *Talks*. In the discourse which follows here, sentences were extracted from numerous talks, as if Ramana were conversing with the reader in response to consistent queries, or as if he were Ashtavakra replying to Janaka's initial question.

How can I be Self-realized?

Ramana:

Transcend your present plane of relativity (duality). The seer is the seen. There must be a unity underlying these two. The (diverging) mind is the cause of the dualistic idea—the wrong notion of limited (embodied) "self," and the misery consequent on such an erroneous idea. Enlightenment lies beyond relative (dualistic) knowledge. It is absolute.

The "I" thought is the (separative) all-important thought. After the rising up of this I-thought, all other thoughts arise (as "not-I"). The I-thought is therefore the root thought. The perception of "I" is associated with a form, such as the body.

Find out who this "I" is. Wherefrom is the I-thought? Probe into it. Give up the notion that I am "this" thing or "that" thing. When "I" is given up, that is Realization.

"I am this" or "I am that" is the ego. What means "subsidence of the ego"?: to merge into the source of its origin. The reaching of the source of the

I-thought is the destruction of the ego; it is the attainment of the goal, enlightenment.

Identification with the Absolute is another name for the destruction of the ego. "Surrender" is to merge into the Source of the ego.

The ego identifies itself with limitations; so the body is considered separate, and the world separate. The birth of the ego is called the birth of the "person." See wherefrom the ego arises.

Uncertainties, doubts and fears are inseparable from the ego. When the ego goes, they go with it.

What *is* the ego: inquire. So long as one does not look closely, it continues to give trouble. How it is to be looked for is learned from those (Self-realized) who have already done so.

Your ego and your mind are the same. The mind is only a projection from the Self. What lies beyond the ego (and mind) is the Self.

If you try to locate the mind, the mind vanishes and the Self alone remains. What you call "mind" is an illusion. It has its beginning with the I-thought. Whose mind is it? The ego's. Is the ego real? No.

The feeling of limitation (separation) is the work of the mind. What is mind? Find it. If you search for it, it will vanish by itself. For it has no real existence.

Mind and ideas are the factors of your wrong identity. The "individual" confines himself to the limits of the changeful body or of the mind—

which derives existence from the unchanging Self. All that is necessary is to give up this mistaken identity; and that done, the Self will be seen to be the single, nondual Reality.

Thoughts comprise the mind. Searching for what the mind is...the seeker will know that thoughts arise from the Self. It is the aggregate of these thoughts that we call "mind." Thoughts are not real: the only reality is the Self.

"The body is I" is the error. This false sense of "I" must go. The *real* I is always there. It is *here* and *now*. The Self is unlimited, and is not confined to the body. There is always only one, and that is the Self.

The Self has no form. The trouble is...you think that you are the body, or that you are mind... which are both changing and transient. But what *you* are is unchanging and eternal. That is what you should know.

The "I" is first created, and then the "world." It is only the "individual" mind that "sees" the world. When this mind disappears (e.g., in death), the world also disappears.

Do you not create a "world" in your dreams? The waking state ("life") is also a long, drawn-out dream. A dreamer dreams a dream. But then he wakes up, and loses all interest in the dream world. So it is with the waking-state world also: "I" and the "world"...are created, have their being, and later vanish.

What is the world? What is *immanent* in it? It is That (the Absolute).

Know your "mind": *then* "see" the world. You will realize that it is not different from the Self. It is unreal, if viewed as apart from the Self; and real, if viewed *as* the Self. (Otherwise) an illusory "being" watches an illusory "world."

You are not being instructed to shut your eyes to this world. You are only to know yourself first, and then see the whole world as the Self.

There is only one, infinite Self. Realize your Self, and then all is realized.

The Self must be realized, which is the same as realizing God. There is no difference between God and Self. You now think that you are an individual, and that there is a universe, and that God is beyond the cosmos. So there is the idea of *separateness*. This idea must go. For God is not separate from you or the cosmos.

Do not delude yourself by imagining God outside of you. God is in all, *and* in the "seer." Being immanent everywhere, there is no particular place for God. The fact is that God is all: there is nothing apart.

So, find who "you" are, and then you may find if God is distinct from you. After finding *who* you are, you may see what God is.

There is only Being. There is no you, or I, or "other." The Self is ever the witness ("seer" of all that's seen), whether so imagined or not. The Self is the basis of all that's experienced. It remains as the "witness" and the support of them all. When the object "witnessed" and the "witness" finally merge together, the Absolute consciousness alone reigns supreme.

The essential aim of the Vedas is to show us that we are That. The instruction is for those who see diversity (duality). After finding the source of the "I," merge your individuality into that Oneness—which is unborn and devoid of all duality. There is One alone, and there is no second.

Being the Self, one remains always "realized." Why should one practice meditation?

Even when the eyes are closed, the mind follows thoughts. When the mind is active, even solitude becomes like a marketplace.

How is It to be contemplated, unless it is *divided* into the "contemplator" and the "contemplated"? No effort is needed to *remain* as the Self. No long process is necessary to know the Self.

Ramana often speaks of three bodily conditions: waking; dreaming; and deep, dreamless sleep. In the latter, we experience no sense of individuality, thus no separativeness. This condition of empty awareness (some scriptures call this pure consciousness) is our "true nature"; the waking and dreaming states (with I-consciousness in both) are superimposed on it, like a film that plays out upon a movie screen. When Ramana says no long process is needed to know the Self, he means that we live without our *small* self on a regular experiential (nightly) basis: the formless nondual condition is actually our "default position." (Wherever he used the word "sleep" he does not mean *dreaming* sleep but *un-conscious* sleep.)

Ramana:

Sleep is unalloyed Self. What happens in sleep is your real nature. That continues now, too. Were you aware of any "form" then?

There is no duality in sleep—whereas, there is duality in the waking state. Deep sleep is simply the state of nonduality.

Can the difference between "individuals" persist there (where there is) forgetfulness of *all* differences? The Self is pure consciousness. There is no awareness of the "body" or of the "world"... of the "individual" and the objects (forms).

What is your state in dreamless sleep? Are you conscious of your "individuality" then? The sleep state is free from thoughts, *and* their impression for the "individual."

How were you in deep sleep? There was no thought of being a "man." You were not the "body" in sleep. Are "you" the body now? Find out; then the whole problem is solved. We do not think of the body, or "God," or the means to Realization in our deep slumber.

Just see what happens in sleep. There is no "ego," no "world," no "seeker," no "guru," etc. There was no I-thought in sleep.

In deep sleep, there were no objects, no "witness," etc. There is no feeling, thinking, etc., in sleep and yet there is *being*. In sleep, there is no "mind."

Why do questions arise now, and not in sleep? Do *any* questions arise in your sleep? The fact is that you have no limitations in sleep, and no question arises. Your (true) consciousness, when asleep, is the same as that when awake.

Did you ask, while asleep, "where do I go after death?" Why raise these questions relating to events after death? They will not be raised sometime hence, when you fall asleep. Before considering what happens after death, just consider what happens in your sleep.... It is the body which was born, and it is that which will die. Anything *created* will certainly be *destroyed*.

The Eternal is not born, nor does it die. When you cease to identify your self with the body, and see the real Self, this confusion will vanish: the "obstacles" are at an end, and samadhi results; that is, Peace reigns.

Samadhi means "the deep-sleep state while in the waking state." The state of sahaja samadhi, that is Realization, for sure.

The Self is certainly within the direct experience of everyone—but not as one *imagines* it to be. It is only "as it is." This (realization) experience is samadhi.

Samadhi is one's own true nature. Samadhi is one's natural state. The ever-present state is the natural state, sahaja.

Samadhi alone can reveal the truth. Thoughts cast a veil over Reality, and so it cannot be clear in states *other* than samadhi....

The egoless "I am" is not thought. It is realization.

In sahaja, the mind has resolved itself into the Self; "differences" and "obstructions" do not, therefore, exist there. When the one who asks about the nature of samadhi—and the "method" of getting into it—vanishes, samadhi is the result.

A strong conviction is necessary that "I am the Self," *transcending* the mind and any phenomena.

What is samadhi? Samadhi is one's essential nature. How, then, can it "come" or "go"?

Remaining in the primal, pure natural state without effort is sahaja samadhi. Samadhi transcends the "mind." You will know only when you are in samadhi.

There is no difference in the samadhi state or in jnana (Self-realization). Are we separate? No, says the jnani (Self-realized).

The jnani's mind remains ever in eternal Peace. He is not aware of anything other than the Self. He knows by his experience that he is not bound by any kind of limitations.

The jnani himself knows the Truth, and is not confused.... In the state of jnana, the jnani sees nothing separate from the Self.... Therefore there is not even jnana, as it is commonly understood. The ordinary ideas of jnana are relative, thus false. The true state is only that of the nondual Self. It is eternal, and abides whether one is aware of it *or not*.

References

ASHTAVAKRA GITA

The first figure given, after a verse, is its chapter number; the second figure is the verse number. The first sentence of each section is given, and then the following references for that section.

Do not find any duality 2-21; 18-40; 18-72; 18-57; 15-15; 18-82; 17-15; 2-16.

The wise are free of imaginings 18-53; 18-7; 10-2; 18-1.

All this time, I have been duped by illusion 2-1; 1-12; 2-23; 2-7.

All this is the product of illusion, and nothing exists 18-70; 18-28; 5-3; 2-24; 2-18; 15-17; 11-8.

The wise one is unattached to the objects of this world 3-8; 3-2; 9-1; 3-11.

As the same all-pervading air 1-20; 3-5; 1-19; 2-6; 2-4; 2-5; 2-10.

The Self is absolute 18-5; 1-12; 15-9; 12-2; 4-6; 3-3; 16-2; 15-18; 20-4; 20-13; 1-16; 7-2; 7-5; 6-4; 18-78.

The wise one lives without the feeling of I-ness, mine-ness 18-73; 20-3; 17-19; 2-25.

Egoism says "I am the doer" 1-8; 11-6; 16-10; 17-19; 18-25.

Give up self-modification 1-18; 13-5; 11-7; 15-10.

You are the One seer of all 1-7; 1-5; 1-12; 1-3; 15-4.

Because he desires to become It, the seeker does not attain it 8-37; 10-3; 18-67.

The sage is without motive 18-64; 12-5; 18-23; 6-1; 18-41.

The sage is not distracted even in "distraction" 18-97; 18-14.

The seeker does not attain liberation through activity by way of repeated practice 18-36; 18-33; 18-45; 15-20.

The one who knows That for certain becomes free from the conflict of thought, and peaceful 11-7; 5-5.

Rules of conduct, renunciation, and restraint—what are they to one who is of the nature of That? 18-71; 4-4; 18-84; 15-2.

Contentment ever dwells in the heart of the wise one who lives with whatever comes to him 18-85; 18-89; 18-82; 18-94; 18-93; 18-8; 18-27; 18-65; 18-22; 18-55; 4-2; 18-100; 18-39; 18-42; 9-8; 18-59; 9-6; 18-70; 5-4.

"Parts" have no significance for the one who has transcended such dual notions as "this is" and "this is not" 18-12; 20-2; 18-16; 20-6; 16-8; 13-6; 17-18; 20-12; 17-1; 18-82; 18-84; 11-7; 8-4; 11-8.

A wise person will gain enlightenment even by instruction that is casually imparted 15-1; 18-1; 18-6; 18-8; 17-13; 18-68; 16-9; 17-2; 10-4; 11-2; 17-20; 2-17; 18-5; 18-9; 18-98.

You are the Self 15-8; 14-3; 18-47; 18-34; 5-2; 18-95; 15-13; 8-4; 18-11; 18-24; 14-4; 18-56.

Realizing the Self in all—and all in the Self—and free from egoism, and the sense of "mine," he is happy 15-6; 17-7; 19-5; 18-99; 19-8; 18-86; 17-14; 15-10; 15-3.

RAMANA

The number is the numbered talk as given in the source book, not the page number in *Talks*.

Transcend your present plane of relativity, 25, 500, 25, 196, 197, 202, 363, 581.

"I am this" or "I am that" is the ego. 363, 129, 130, 201, 177, 251, 612.

Your ego and your mind are the same, 195, 76, 81, 217, 238, 328, 610, 616.

Thoughts comprise the mind, 326, 211.

"The body is I" is the error, 96, 144, 164, 653.

The "I" is first created, and then the "world," 454, 556, 487, 625, 641, 639, 53, 516, 443, 272, 20.

The Self must be realized, which is the same as realizing God, 90, 199, 649, 208, 244, 270, 602, 439, 17, 137, 617, 68, 30, 264, 448, 77.

Being the Self, one remains always "realized," 462, 539, 542, 204, 66, 647.

Sleep is unalloyed Self, 344, 304, 502, 207, 609, 176, 609, 601, 426, 269.

Just see what happens in sleep 363, 222, 143, 295, 566.

Why do questions arise now, and not in sleep? 242, 565, 354,13, 258, 242, 426, 238, 238, 276.

Samadhi means "the deep-sleep state while in the waking state," 372, 57,141, 199, 136,17, 226,187,155, 406, 249, 597, 391,110.

There is no difference in the samadhi state or in jnana 256, 398,139,158, 513, 499.

Robert Wolfe

www.livingnonduality.org
robert@livingnonduality.org

c/o Karina Library Press
P.O. Box 35
Ojai, California 93024

To leave a review and help others discover
this work: *amzn.com/1937902129*

86388435R00042

Made in the USA
Lexington, KY
11 April 2018